Empowered Through Chaos

Ethan A. Robbins

Published by Ethan A. Robbins, 2024.

EMPOWERED THROUGH CHAOS

First edition. July 31, 2024.

ISBN: 979-8227120472

Written by Ethan A. Robbins.

Also by Ethan A. Robbins

Empowered Through Chaos

Table of Contents

EMPOWERED Through Chaos
Harnessing Resilience in Turbulent Times

By

PREFACE

In an era marked by rapid change and unprecedented challenges, the journey to resilience has never been more crucial. **"Empowered Through Chaos: Harnessing Resilience in Turbulent Times"** is a testament to the indomitable human spirit that thrives in the face of adversity. This book is not just a collection of strategies and insights; it is a lifeline for anyone seeking to navigate the tumultuous waters of life with strength and grace.

As a motivational speaker and life coach, I have had the privilege of witnessing firsthand the remarkable transformations that occur when individuals embrace their inner resilience. From the boardroom to the living room, the principles of resilience are universally applicable, providing a foundation upon which we can all build a more empowered existence.

This book is divided into chapters that explore the various facets of resilience, from understanding its psychological underpinnings to practical, actionable advice that you can implement immediately. Together, we will journey through real-life examples of resilient women throughout history to uncover the hidden reserves of strength that lie within each of us.

"Empowered Through Chaos" is designed to be more than a reading experience; it is a journey of self-discovery and empowerment. Each chapter is crafted to provide not only theoretical insights but also practical exercises and reflections that will help you apply these principles to your own life. Whether you are facing personal struggles, professional setbacks, or the everyday challenges of an ever-changing world, this book will be your guide, your companion, and your source of inspiration.

May this book ignite a spark of resilience within you and empower you to rise above the chaos with unwavering strength. Your journey to resilience begins now.

Motivational Quote

"In the chaos of life, your greatest power lies not in avoiding the storm, but in learning to dance in the rain. Embrace your resilience, for it is the beacon that will guide you through the darkest of times."

Ethan A. Robbins

By embedding these principles into your daily life, you will discover that resilience is not a destination but a journey—a continuous process of growth, adaptation, and empowerment. Welcome to **"Empowered Through Chaos."** Your resilient path awaits.

INTRODUCTION

Life is an unpredictable journey, often filled with unexpected twists and turns. In these moments of uncertainty and chaos, the strength we seek lies not in avoiding challenges but in our ability to rise and thrive amidst them. "Empowered Through Chaos: Harnessing Resilience in Turbulent Times" is your beacon of hope and empowerment, designed to guide you through your darkest moments and steer you towards a life of unwavering strength and resilience.

The Book's Purpose

WE HAVE CRAFTED THIS book to serve as more than just a guide; it is a companion, a mentor, and a source of inspiration. Here, you will find practical advice, heartfelt stories, and actionable strategies that will empower you to build and nurture your resilience. Whether you are facing personal challenges, professional setbacks, or simply navigating the everyday uncertainties of life, this book offers the tools and insights you need to emerge stronger and more empowered.

What you can expect

THROUGHOUT THIS JOURNEY, you will:

Uncover Inner Strength: Learn to tap into the deep reservoir of strength that resides within you. Through self-reflection and mindfulness exercises, you will discover your true potential and the remarkable resilience you possess.

Cultivate Self-Love: embrace practices that nurture your mind, body, and spirit. Self-love is the cornerstone of resilience, and this book provides you with the techniques to cultivate it daily.

Build an Inner Fortress: Develop strategies to fortify your courage and bolster your strength. From creating a supportive network to adopting a growth mindset, you will learn how to build an unshakeable foundation.

Transform Challenges into Opportunities: See adversity through a new lens, recognizing each challenge as an opportunity for growth and empowerment. This shift in perspective is key to thriving in chaotic times.

Understanding Resilience

MORE THAN JUST OVERCOMING adversity, resilience is the ability to adapt, grow, and thrive. It involves a dynamic process of building mental, emotional, and physical fortitude. At its core, resilience is about embracing change, learning from experiences, and continuously evolving.

In today's fast-paced and ever-changing world, resilience has become an essential skill. Research shows that resilient individuals are not only better equipped to handle stress and recover from setbacks, but they also tend to experience greater overall well-being and success. By developing resilience, you empower yourself to face life's uncertainties with confidence and grace.

Actionable advice for building resilience

Practice Mindfulness: Incorporate mindfulness techniques such as meditation, deep breathing, and journaling into your daily routine. These practices help you stay present, manage stress, and maintain a balanced perspective.

Foster Connections: Build and maintain strong relationships with family, friends, and the community. Social support is a critical component of resilience, providing you with encouragement and a sense of belonging.

Set Realistic Goals: Break down your goals into manageable steps and celebrate small victories along the way. This approach keeps you motivated and focused, even when faced with setbacks.

Embrace Change: View change as an opportunity for growth rather than a threat. By adopting a flexible mindset, you can navigate transitions more smoothly and discover new possibilities in unexpected situations.

Prioritize Self-Care: Take care of your physical health through regular exercise, a balanced diet, and sufficient sleep. A healthy body supports a resilient mind.

As you embark on this journey of resilience, remember that you are not alone. "Empowered Through Chaos" is here to support and guide you every step of the way. Embrace the wisdom, tools, and strategies shared in these pages and discover the resilient woman you were always meant to be. Your journey to rise and thrive begins now.

Workbook for Practical Application

To ensure that the lessons and strategies outlined in this book are effectively implemented in your daily life, we have included a comprehensive workbook at the end of this book. This workbook is designed to help you put theory into practice through guided exercises, reflective prompts, and actionable steps. It will serve as a practical tool to reinforce your learning, track your progress, and solidify your resilience-building journey. By engaging with the workbook, you will gain deeper insights, develop stronger habits, and truly embody the resilience you seek.

CHAPTER ONE

Understanding Resilience

Resilience is a remarkable trait, a powerful force that enables individuals to overcome adversity, adapt to change, and emerge stronger from life's challenges. It is our psychological armor that equips us to face the unpredictable nature of existence with courage and fortitude. In this chapter, we will delve into the definition of resilience, explore its psychological underpinnings, and highlight real-life examples of resilient women throughout history. Our aim is to provide you with actionable advice and genuine value, helping you to cultivate resilience in your own life.

Defining Resilience

At its core, resilience is the ability to bounce back from adversity, trauma, or significant sources of stress. It is not merely about surviving difficulties but thriving despite them. Resilient individuals possess a set of adaptive behaviors, thoughts, and actions that allow them to cope with and recover from setbacks. The American Psychological Association defines resilience as "the process of adapting well in the face of adversity, trauma, tragedy, threats, or significant sources of stress" (APA, 2012).

Resilience is not a fixed trait; it is a dynamic process that can be developed and strengthened over time. It involves a combination of internal factors such as self-esteem, optimism, and emotional regulation, as well as external factors like social support and community resources. Understanding and cultivating these elements can significantly enhance one's capacity for resilience.

The Psychological Underpinnings of Resilience

Resilience is deeply rooted in several psychological theories and concepts:

Cognitive Appraisal Theory:

This theory posits that how we perceive and interpret a stressful event significantly impacts our emotional and behavioral response to it. Resilient individuals tend to view challenges as opportunities for growth rather than insurmountable obstacles. They engage in positive reappraisal, reframing negative experiences in a more constructive light.

Self-Efficacy:

Coined by psychologist Albert Bandura, self-efficacy refers to an individual's belief in their ability to influence events that affect their lives. High self-efficacy is associated with greater resilience as it fosters a proactive approach to problem-solving and coping with stress.

Emotional Regulation:

The ability to manage and modulate emotional responses is crucial for resilience. Techniques such as mindfulness, meditation, and cognitive-behavioral strategies can enhance emotional regulation, enabling individuals to stay calm and focused under pressure.

Social Support:

A robust network of supportive relationships provides emotional comfort, practical assistance, and a sense of belonging. Social support acts as a buffer against stress, enhancing resilience by reducing the perceived impact of adversity.

Growth Mindset:

Popularized by psychologist Carol Dweck, a growth mindset is the belief that abilities and intelligence can be developed through dedication and hard work. This mindset encourages resilience by promoting a love for learning, a willingness to take on challenges, and the perseverance to overcome obstacles.

Real-life Examples of Resilient Women Throughout History

THE ANNALS OF HISTORY are replete with stories of women who have exemplified resilience in the face of formidable challenges. These women serve as powerful role models, demonstrating that resilience is not confined to a particular era or circumstance.

Harriet Tubman:

Born into slavery, Harriet Tubman escaped to freedom and became a leading abolitionist, guiding hundreds of enslaved people to freedom via the Underground Railroad. Her resilience was evident in her unwavering commitment to justice and her extraordinary courage in the face of immense danger.

Malala Yousafzai:

A Pakistani activist for female education, Malala Yousafzai, survived a brutal assassination attempt by the Taliban. Despite this life-threatening ordeal, she continued to advocate for girls' education worldwide, earning the Nobel Peace Prize in 2001. Malala's resilience shines through her dedication to her cause and her ability to transform personal trauma into global activism.

Marie Curie:

A pioneering scientist, Marie Curie faced numerous obstacles, including gender discrimination and personal loss. Despite these challenges, she made groundbreaking contributions to the field of radioactivity, becoming the first woman to win a Nobel Prize and the only person to win Nobel Prizes in two different scientific fields. Curie's resilience was rooted in her relentless pursuit of knowledge and her ability to persevere through adversity.

Oprah Winfrey:

Overcoming a childhood marked by poverty and abuse, Oprah Winfrey became one of the most influential media moguls in the world. Her resilience is reflected in her ability to rise above her circumstances, build a successful career, and use her platform to inspire and empower others.

Actionable Advice for Building Resilience

BUILDING RESILIENCE is a proactive process that involves intentional effort and practice. Here are some actionable tips to help you develop resilience:

Cultivate a Positive Outlook

Practice gratitude and positive thinking. Focus on the things you can control and find meaning in your experiences, even the difficult ones.

Develop Strong Relationships

Nurture your connections with family, friends, and the community. Seek support when needed and offer it to others, creating a network of mutual aid.

Embrace Change:

Accept that change is a part of life. View setbacks as opportunities to learn and grow. Flexibility and adaptability are key components of resilience.

Practice Self-Care:

Prioritize your physical, emotional, and mental well-being. Engage in regular exercise, maintain a healthy diet, and practice mindfulness or relaxation techniques.

Set Realistic Goals

Break your goals into manageable steps and celebrate small achievements along the way. This approach helps build confidence and motivation.

Learn from Experience

Reflect on past experiences and identify the strategies that helped you cope. Use this knowledge to handle future challenges more effectively.

By understanding the psychological foundations of resilience and drawing inspiration from the resilient women who have come before us, you can embark on your journey to becoming a more resilient individual. Remember, resilience is not about being invincible; it is about being adaptable, persistent, and strong in the face of adversity.

CHAPTER ONE

The Power of Self-Discovery

Self-discovery is a transformative journey that reveals our core essence, unlocks our true potential, and empowers us to live more authentically. It's a process of introspection and revelation that allows us to understand our strengths, values, and passions, leading to a more fulfilled and purpose-driven life. In this chapter, we'll explore effective techniques for self-reflection, practical exercises to uncover your inner potential, and actionable advice to help you on this enlightening journey.

Techniques for Self-Reflection

Journaling for Clarity

One of the most profound ways to engage in self-reflection is through journaling. This practice involves writing down your thoughts, feelings, and experiences, which can provide valuable insights into your inner world. To get started, set aside a quiet time each day to journal. Focus on topics such as your goals, challenges, and daily experiences. Ask yourself questions like, "What am I passionate about?" or "What accomplishments am I most proud of?" Regular journaling can help you track patterns, recognize personal growth, and clarify your aspirations.

Mindfulness Meditation

Mindfulness meditation is another powerful technique for self-reflection. Practice mindfulness to train your mind to focus on the present moment without judgment. This practice can help you gain deeper insights into your thoughts and emotions. To begin, find a quiet space, sit comfortably, and focus on your breath. When thoughts arise, gently acknowledge them and return to your breath. Over time, mindfulness can enhance your self-awareness and help you understand your reactions and emotional triggers.

Strengths Assessment

Identifying your strengths is crucial for personal growth. Tools such as the StrengthsFinder assessment can provide a comprehensive understanding of your natural talents and abilities. These assessments often categorize strengths into specific themes, allowing you to gain insights into areas where you excel. After discovering your strengths, use them in your career, relationships, and personal projects.

Exercises to discover your inner potential

THE LIFE TIMELINE EXERCISE

Creating a life timeline is an effective way to uncover your inner potential. Start by drawing a horizontal line on a piece of paper, marking significant events in your life along the timeline. Include both positive and negative experiences, such as achievements, challenges, and turning points. Reflect on how these events have shaped you and what lessons you've learned. This exercise can help you recognize patterns, understand your growth trajectory, and identify areas where you have demonstrated resilience and strength.

The "5 Whys" Technique

The "5 Whys" technique is a simple yet powerful tool for exploring the underlying reasons behind your goals and desires. Begin by stating a goal or aspiration, then ask yourself "why" this goal is important. For each answer you provide, ask "why" again, repeating this process until you reach the core motivation behind your goal. This technique can help you gain a deeper understanding of your true desires and align your actions with your core values.

Visualizing Your Ideal Self

Visualization is a technique used by many successful individuals to manifest their goals and aspirations. To use this technique for self-discovery, find a quiet space and close your eyes. Imagine yourself living your ideal life, achieving your dreams, and embodying your highest potential. Details of this vision—what are you doing, feeling, and with whom? This exercise can help you clarify your goals, identify the steps needed to achieve them, and cultivate a sense of purpose and motivation.

Seeking Feedback

Gaining insights from others can provide valuable perspectives on your strengths and areas for improvement. Reach out to trusted friends, family members, or colleagues and ask them for constructive feedback. You can frame your questions around specific aspects of your personality, work habits, or skills. For example, you might ask, "What do you think are my greatest strengths?" or "In what areas do you see the most potential for growth?" Be open to their observations, and use their feedback to enhance your self-awareness and development.

Actionable advice for continuous growth

SET REALISTIC GOALS

Setting achievable goals is essential for applying your self-discovery insights. Break down your larger aspirations into smaller, manageable steps and create a timeline for accomplishing them. Use the SMART criteria—specific, measurable, achievable, relevant, and time-bound—to ensure your goals are clear and attainable. Regularly review and adjust your goals as needed, and celebrate your progress along the way.

Embrace Lifelong Learning

Self-discovery is an ongoing journey, and embracing lifelong learning can help you continue growing and evolving. Pursue opportunities for personal and professional development, such as workshops, courses, or reading. Stay curious and open to new experiences, as they can provide fresh insights and expand your understanding of yourself.

Practice Self-Compassion

Self-discovery can sometimes uncover uncomfortable truths or areas where you feel inadequate. It's important to practice self-compassion and treat yourself with kindness and understanding. Acknowledge your imperfections and recognize that growth is a continuous process. When you are gentle with yourself, you create a supportive environment for personal development.

Build a Supportive Network

Surround yourself with individuals who inspire and support your growth. A strong support network can provide encouragement, accountability, and diverse perspectives. Engage with mentors, join groups aligned with your interests, and connect with like-minded individuals who share your values and aspirations.

The power of self-discovery lies in its ability to illuminate your true potential and guide you towards a more authentic and fulfilling life. By employing techniques such as journaling, mindfulness meditation, and strengths assessments, you can gain valuable insights into your inner world. Engaging in exercises like the life timeline, "5 Whys," and visualization can help you uncover and embrace your unique strengths and aspirations. With actionable advice for setting goals, embracing lifelong learning, and practicing self-compassion, you can continue your journey of self-discovery with confidence and clarity. Embrace the process, and let your inner potential guide you towards a life of purpose and fulfillment.

CHAPTER TWO

The Power of Self-Discovery

Self-discovery is more than just a personal journey; it's a profound exploration into the essence of who you are, what drives you, and how you can leverage your inherent strengths to achieve a fulfilling life. This chapter will delve into effective techniques for self-reflection and understanding your strengths, as well as practical exercises to uncover your inner potential. By integrating these approaches into your life, you can gain deeper insights, unlock new opportunities, and align your actions with your true self.

Techniques for Self-Reflection and Understanding Your Strengths

R eflective Journaling
Journaling is a time-honored technique that provides a mirror for your inner thoughts and emotions. To get started, find a quiet place and dedicate a few minutes each day to writing. Focus on various aspects of your life, such as recent experiences, challenges, and achievements. Pose reflective questions like, "What moments made me feel most alive?" or "When did I feel most confident?" Over time, you'll notice patterns and insights emerging, revealing your core strengths and areas for growth. Make it a habit to review your entries periodically to track your progress and evolving understanding.

Assessments of Personality and Strength

Utilizing personality and strengths assessments can provide structured insights into your natural tendencies and abilities. Tools like the Myers-Briggs Type Indicator (MBTI) or the StrengthsFinder assessment categorize your traits and talents, offering a comprehensive overview of your personality profile. These assessments help you understand how your unique attributes align with various roles and environments. After completing an assessment, reflect on the results and consider how you can apply your strengths in both personal and professional contexts.

Mindfulness and Self-awareness

Mindfulness practices foster a deeper connection with your inner self by promoting present-moment awareness. Incorporate mindfulness exercises such as meditation, breathing techniques, or mindful walking into your routine. Start with just a few minutes each day, focusing on observing your thoughts and feelings without judgment. This practice helps you become more aware of your emotional responses and thought patterns, enhancing your ability to understand and manage your strengths and weaknesses effectively.

Feedback from Others

Seeking feedback from trusted friends, family, or colleagues can provide external perspectives on your strengths and areas for improvement. Create a list of people whose opinions you value, and ask them specific questions about your skills and characteristics. For example, "What do you think are my greatest strengths?" or "In which areas do you see potential for growth?" Use their insights to gain a broader understanding of how you are perceived and to identify areas where you can enhance your capabilities.

Exercises to Discover Your Inner Potential

THE LIST OF LIFE ACHIEVEMENTS

Creating a life achievement list is a powerful exercise for recognizing and celebrating your accomplishments. Start by listing significant achievements in various areas of your life, such as career, personal development, relationships, and hobbies. Include both major milestones and smaller victories. Reflect on these achievements to identify common themes and skills that contributed to your success. This exercise can help you pinpoint your strengths and motivate you to pursue further opportunities that align with your abilities.

Vision Board Creation

A vision board is a visual representation of your goals and aspirations. To create one, gather magazines, printouts, or other materials that resonate with your dreams and desires. Cut out images, words, or phrases that represent your goals and values. Arrange them on a board or poster, and place them in a visible location. Regularly update your vision board to reflect new goals and aspirations. This exercise helps clarify your vision, align your actions with your goals, and maintain motivation as you work towards achieving them.

Personal SWOT Analysis

A SWOT analysis (Strengths, Weaknesses, Opportunities, and Threats) is a strategic tool used to assess various aspects of your personal and professional life. Create a SWOT matrix by listing your strengths, weaknesses, opportunities, and threats. Reflect on each category to gain a comprehensive understanding of your capabilities and challenges. Use this analysis to develop strategies for leveraging your strengths, addressing your weaknesses, seizing opportunities, and mitigating potential threats. This exercise provides actionable insights for personal development and goal-setting.

Passion and Purposeful Exploration

Exploring your passions and purpose is essential for uncovering your inner potential. Start by listing activities, subjects, or causes that ignite your enthusiasm. Reflect on why these passions resonate with you and how they align with your values and long-term goals. Consider how you can incorporate these passions into your daily life, career, or personal projects. This exercise helps you align your actions with your core values, leading to a more fulfilling and purpose-driven life.

Actionable Tips for Applying Self-Discovery Insights

SET SMART GOALS

Once you've gained insights into your strengths and passions, set SMART (specific, measurable, achievable, relevant, and time-bound) goals to turn your discoveries into actionable steps. For example, if you've identified a passion for writing, a SMART goal might be, "Write 500 words a day for the next three months to complete a manuscript." Setting clear and achievable goals helps you stay focused and motivated, turning your self-discovery into tangible progress.

Create an Action Plan

Develop an action plan outlining the steps you need to take to achieve your goals. Break down your goals into smaller, manageable tasks and assign deadlines for each step. Regularly review and adjust your action plan as needed, and track your progress to stay on course. An action plan provides a structured approach to applying your insights and ensures that you make consistent progress towards your aspirations.

Practice Self-care and Reflection

Self-discovery is an ongoing process that requires regular self-care and reflection. Prioritize activities that nurture your well-being, such as exercise, relaxation, and hobbies. Schedule time for regular self-reflection, whether through journaling, meditation, or simply taking a quiet walk. By maintaining a balanced and reflective approach, you create a supportive environment for continued personal growth and self-discovery.

Seek Support and Mentorship

Engaging with mentors or support networks can enhance your self-discovery journey. Seek guidance from individuals who have experience in areas you are passionate about or who can offer valuable perspectives. Participate in communities or groups aligned with your interests and goals. Surrounding yourself with supportive and inspiring individuals can provide motivation, accountability, and valuable insights as you continue to explore and develop your potential.

The power of self-discovery lies in its ability to unlock your true potential and guide you towards a more authentic and purposeful life. By employing techniques such as reflective journaling, strengths assessments, and mindfulness practices, you can gain valuable insights into your inner self. Engaging in exercises like the Life Achievement List, Vision Board Creation, and Personal SWOT Analysis helps you uncover and embrace your unique strengths and aspirations. With actionable tips for setting goals, creating action plans, and seeking support, you can apply your self-discovery insights to achieve meaningful progress and live a fulfilling life. Embrace the journey of self-discovery, and let it empower you to reach your highest potential.

CHAPTER THREE

Nurturing Self-Love

Self-love is a foundational element for personal well-being and resilience. It is the practice of recognizing and valuing your own worth, treating yourself with kindness, and fostering a positive self-image. In this chapter, we will explore the importance of self-love in building resilience and delve into practical practices for cultivating self-compassion and positive self-talk. By implementing these strategies, you can enhance your emotional resilience, foster a healthier self-relationship, and navigate life's challenges with greater ease.

The Importance of Self-Love in Building Resilience

The foundation for Emotional Strength

Self-love is essential for developing emotional resilience, which is the ability to adapt and bounce back from adversity. When you cultivate self-love, you build a strong foundation of self-worth and confidence. This internal strength enables you to face challenges with a positive mindset, knowing that you have inherent value regardless of external circumstances. Self-love helps you maintain a balanced perspective, allowing you to navigate setbacks without losing sight of your worth or potential.

Healthy Boundaries and Self-Advocacy

A key aspect of self-love is setting and maintaining healthy boundaries. When you value yourself, you recognize the importance of protecting your well-being and ensuring that your needs are met. This involves advocating for yourself, saying no when necessary, and prioritizing your own health and happiness. Healthy boundaries prevent burnout and promote a sense of empowerment, enabling you to handle stressors more effectively and maintain a resilient mindset.

Positive Self-Perception

Self-love fosters a positive self-perception, which is crucial for resilience. By affirming your worth and acknowledging your achievements, you reinforce a positive self-image. This self-assurance acts as a buffer against negative self-talk and external criticism. A positive self-perception encourages you to approach challenges with optimism and perseverance, as you trust in your ability to overcome obstacles and achieve your goals.

Practices for Cultivating Self-Compassion

SELF-COMPASSIONATE Journaling

Self-compassionate journaling is a powerful practice for nurturing self-love and understanding. Begin by writing a letter to yourself as if you were writing to a dear friend. Acknowledge any difficulties you are facing and offer yourself words of encouragement, kindness, and understanding. Reflect on your strengths and past successes, and remind yourself of your worth. This practice helps shift your mindset from self-criticism to self-acceptance, fostering a more compassionate relationship with yourself.

Mindfulness Meditation for Self-Compassion

Mindfulness meditation can enhance self-compassion by helping you develop a non-judgmental awareness of your thoughts and feelings. Set aside time each day for mindfulness practice. Sit comfortably, close your eyes, and focus on your breath. As thoughts and emotions arise, observe them without judgment and gently return your focus to your breath. Incorporate self-compassionate phrases, such as "May I be kind to myself" or "May I accept myself as I am," to reinforce a compassionate mindset. This practice helps you cultivate a loving and understanding attitude toward yourself.

Forgiveness Practices

Forgiveness is a crucial aspect of self-compassion. Often, we hold onto past mistakes or regrets, which can hinder our self-love. Practice self-forgiveness by acknowledging any past errors or shortcomings and recognizing that they do not define your worth. Write a letter of forgiveness to yourself, expressing understanding and releasing any self-judgment. This exercise helps you let go of guilt and shame, allowing you to embrace your humanity and move forward with compassion.

Techniques for Positive Self-Talk

AFFIRMATIONS FOR SELF-Love

Positive affirmations are statements that reinforce self-love and confidence. Create a list of affirmations that resonate with you, such as "I am worthy of love and respect" or "I believe in my abilities." Repeat these affirmations daily, either aloud or silently, to reinforce a positive self-image. Place your affirmations in visible locations, such as on your mirror or desk, to remind yourself of your inherent value. This practice helps counteract negative self-talk and cultivates a more positive and loving inner dialogue.

Challenging Negative Self-talk

Identifying and challenging negative self-talk is essential for fostering positive self-beliefs. Pay attention to the negative thoughts that arise and question their validity. Ask yourself if these thoughts are based on facts or assumptions. Replace negative thoughts with more balanced and positive statements. For example, if you think, "I'm not talented enough," counter it with, "I have strengths and abilities that contribute to my success." This technique helps shift your mindset from self-doubt to self-affirmation.

Gratitude Practices

Gratitude practices can enhance positive self-talk by shifting your focus towards what you appreciate about yourself. Each day, make a list of qualities or achievements you are grateful for. This could include personal attributes, skills, or accomplishments. Reflect on these items and acknowledge their significance in your life. Practicing gratitude helps you recognize and celebrate your strengths, fostering a more positive and loving self-perception.

Visualization Techniques

Visualization is a technique used to create a mental image of your ideal self and future goals. To practice visualization, find a quiet space and close your eyes. Picture yourself achieving your goals and embodying the qualities you aspire to have. Imagine the positive emotions and experiences that accompany this vision. Visualization helps reinforce a positive self-image and motivates you to take actions aligned with your aspirations. It also strengthens your self-belief and resilience by providing a clear mental picture of your potential.

Actionable advice for nurturing self-love

CREATE A SELF-LOVE Routine

Establish a daily or weekly routine dedicated to self-love practices. This might include activities such as journaling, mindfulness meditation, or engaging in hobbies you enjoy. Incorporate self-care practices that nurture your physical, emotional, and mental well-being. Making self-love a regular part of your routine reinforces its importance and creates a consistent foundation for personal growth and resilience.

Build a Support System

Surround yourself with individuals who support and encourage your journey of self-love. Seek out friends, family members, or mentors who uplift you and affirm your worth. Engage in communities or groups that share your values and aspirations. A supportive network provides encouragement, accountability, and positive reinforcement, contributing to your overall self-love and resilience.

Set Realistic Expectations

Set realistic and attainable goals for yourself, and avoid placing undue pressure on yourself to achieve perfection. Embrace the idea that growth and progress are ongoing processes, and allow yourself to make mistakes and learn from them. By setting achievable goals and practicing self-compassion, you create a positive and nurturing environment for personal development and self-love.

Celebrate your Achievements

Regularly celebrate your achievements and milestones, no matter how small. Recognize and acknowledge your successes, and take time to reflect on your accomplishments. Celebrating your achievements reinforces a positive self-image and fosters a sense of pride and self-worth. It also motivates you to continue pursuing your goals with confidence and resilience.

Nurturing self-love is essential for building resilience and fostering a positive relationship with yourself. Understanding the importance of self-love, cultivating self-compassion through practices such as journaling and mindfulness, and implementing techniques for positive self-talk can help you improve your emotional strength and well-being. Embrace the journey of self-love with actionable tips and consistent practices, and let it empower you to face life's challenges with confidence and grace. Self-love is not only about valuing yourself but also about creating a foundation for a resilient and fulfilling life.

CHAPTER FOUR

Building Your Inner Fortress

In the face of life's inevitable challenges, mental and emotional fortitude serve as your inner fortress, safeguarding you against adversity and empowering you to thrive despite obstacles. Building this inner strength involves developing resilience and crafting a robust support system that reinforces your capacity to navigate difficulties. In this chapter, we will explore strategies for developing mental and emotional fortitude and offer practical advice on creating a support system that strengthens your resilience. By integrating these approaches into your life, you can enhance your ability to overcome adversity and achieve a greater sense of well-being and empowerment.

Strategies to Develop Mental and Emotional Fortitude

Embrace a Growth Mindset

A growth mindset is the belief that your abilities and intelligence can be developed through effort, learning, and perseverance. Embracing this mindset allows you to view challenges as opportunities for growth rather than insurmountable obstacles. To cultivate a growth mindset, focus on the process of learning and improvement rather than solely on outcomes. Celebrate your progress, no matter how small, and use setbacks as learning experiences. By adopting a growth mindset, you build mental resilience and maintain a positive outlook even in the face of adversity.

Develop Emotional Awareness

Emotional awareness entails recognizing and understanding your emotions, as well as their impact on your behavior and decisions. Developing this awareness is crucial for managing your emotional responses and building resilience. Practice mindfulness techniques to become more attuned to your emotions and thought patterns. Regularly check in with yourself to identify how you're feeling and why. Journaling about your emotions and experiences can also help you gain insight and manage your emotional state more effectively.

Cultivate Stress-Management Techniques

Effective stress management is essential for maintaining mental and emotional fortitude. Identify stressors in your life and implement techniques to manage them effectively. Techniques such as deep breathing exercises, progressive muscle relaxation, and physical exercise can help reduce stress and promote relaxation. Find activities that you enjoy that help you unwind, such as reading, listening to music, or engaging in hobbies. By incorporating stress management practices into your routine, you enhance your ability to cope with challenges and maintain emotional balance.

Create a Resilience Toolkit

A resilience toolbox is a collection of strategies and resources that you can draw upon during times of stress or adversity. Include practical tools such as coping strategies, positive affirmations, and relaxation techniques. Regularly review and update your toolbox to ensure it reflects your current needs and challenges. By having a well-stocked resilience toolbox, you equip yourself with the tools needed to navigate difficulties and maintain mental and emotional strength.

Practice Self-Reflection and Goal-Setting

Self-reflection and goal-setting are integral to developing mental fortitude. Set aside time for regular self-reflection to assess your progress, identify areas for improvement, and acknowledge your achievements. Use this reflection to set realistic and achievable goals that align with your values and aspirations. Break down larger goals into smaller, manageable steps, and track your progress regularly. Setting and achieving goals enhances your sense of accomplishment and builds confidence, contributing to your overall mental and emotional strength.

How to Create a Support System That Strengthens Resilience

IDENTIFY YOUR SUPPORT Network

Building a strong support system begins with identifying individuals who can offer emotional support, encouragement, and practical assistance. Consider family members, friends, mentors, colleagues, and community members who play a positive role in your life. Make a list of these individuals and evaluate the strengths they bring to your support network. Recognize the value of each person's contribution, and seek to nurture these relationships by maintaining open communication and expressing gratitude for their support.

Foster Meaningful Relationships

To strengthen your support system, focus on building and maintaining meaningful relationships. Invest time and effort in nurturing connections with individuals who share your values and interests. Engage in activities and conversations that deepen your understanding of one another and foster mutual support. Be proactive in reaching out to others, offering support when needed, and celebrating shared successes. Meaningful relationships provide a sense of belonging and reinforce your resilience by offering emotional and practical support.

Seek Professional Guidance

Sometimes, professional guidance is essential for building and maintaining resilience. Consider seeking support from mental health professionals such as therapists, counselors, or coaches. These professionals can provide valuable insights, coping strategies, and tools for managing stress and adversity. They can also help you navigate complex emotions and challenges, offering a neutral perspective and expert guidance. Don't hesitate to reach out for professional support when needed, as it can be a crucial component of a robust support system.

Participate in Support Groups

Support groups offer a sense of community and shared experience, which can be invaluable for building resilience. Look for support groups or communities that align with your interests, challenges, or goals. Participate actively in group discussions, share your experiences, and learn from others. Support groups provide a platform for exchanging ideas, offering and receiving support, and finding encouragement from individuals who understand your situation. Engaging in support groups can enhance your resilience by providing a network of empathetic and supportive individuals.

Cultivate Reciprocity

Building a strong support system involves reciprocity, which means both giving and receiving support. Be an active and engaged member of your support network, offering help, encouragement, and empathy to others. Cultivate a culture of reciprocity by fostering open communication and expressing appreciation for the support you receive. By contributing to others' well-being, you reinforce your own support system and create a mutually beneficial environment that strengthens resilience for everyone involved.

Establish Boundaries

Establishing healthy boundaries is crucial for maintaining a balanced support system. Clearly communicate your needs, limits, and expectations to your support network. Respect your own and others' boundaries to ensure that relationships remain positive and supportive. Safe boundaries prevent burnout, give you time to recharge, and focus on yourself. By setting and maintaining boundaries, you create a supportive environment that fosters resilience and mutual respect.

Actionable Tips for Building Your Inner Fortress

CREATE A RESILIENCE action plan

Develop a resilience action plan outlining the strategies and resources you will use to build and maintain mental and emotional fortitude. Include specific goals, stress management techniques, and tools from your resilience toolbox. Regularly review and update your action plan to reflect changes in your life and evolving needs. A well-structured action plan provides a clear roadmap for developing resilience and navigating challenges effectively.

Engage in Regular Self-care

Prioritize self-care as a key component of building your inner fortress. Incorporate activities into your routine that promote physical, emotional, and mental well-being. Set aside time for relaxation, hobbies, and activities that bring you joy. Maintain a balanced lifestyle and address any signs of stress or burnout to prioritize your health and well-being. Regular self-care reinforces your resilience and ensures that you are equipped to handle life's challenges.

Celebrate your Strengths and Achievements

Recognize and celebrate your strengths and achievements as you build your inner fortress. Regularly reflect on your accomplishments and the qualities that contribute to your resilience. Celebrate milestones and successes, no matter how small, and take pride in your progress. By acknowledging your strengths and achievements, you reinforce a positive self-image and build confidence in your ability to overcome challenges.

Stay connected and engage in the community

Stay connected with your support network and engage in community activities that align with your interests and values. Participate in social events, volunteer opportunities, or group activities that foster a sense of belonging and connection. Building and maintaining social connections enhances your resilience by providing emotional support and a sense of community.

Building your inner fortress involves developing mental and emotional fortitude and creating a robust support system that enhances your resilience.

By embracing a growth mindset, cultivating emotional awareness, and implementing stress management techniques, you strengthen your inner resilience. Creating a support system that includes meaningful relationships, professional guidance, and support groups further reinforces your ability to navigate challenges. Incorporate actionable tips such as creating a resilience action plan, engaging in regular self-care, and celebrating your achievements to build and maintain a resilient mindset. With these strategies in place, you can navigate life's obstacles with greater strength and confidence, empowered by the solid foundation of your inner fortress.

CHAPTER FIVE

Embracing change and uncertainty

Change and uncertainty are inevitable aspects of life that can evoke feelings of fear and resistance. However, learning to adapt to and embrace these elements can open doors to new opportunities and growth. This chapter explores techniques for accepting life's unpredictability and offers inspiring stories of women who have thrived despite the uncertainties they faced. By integrating these strategies into your life, you can transform your approach to change and uncertainty, ultimately fostering resilience and achieving personal growth.

Techniques to Adapt to and Accept Life's Unpredictability

Cultivate Flexibility and Openness

Flexibility is essential for adapting to change. Approach new situations with an open mind and a willingness to explore alternative perspectives. Practice embracing uncertainty by stepping out of your comfort zone and trying new experiences. Being flexible allows you to navigate changes more effectively and see them as opportunities rather than threats. For instance, when faced with unexpected changes, such as a sudden career shift, view it as a chance to acquire new skills and explore different paths rather than a setback.

Focus on What You Can Control

In times of uncertainty, focus on aspects of your life that you can control. Though you can't control external events, you can control your reactions and choices. Identify areas where you can make positive changes and take proactive steps to address them. For example, if you're facing job insecurity, concentrate on enhancing your skills, networking, and exploring new career opportunities. By directing your energy toward controllable factors, you maintain a sense of agency and reduce feelings of helplessness.

Practice Mindfulness and Acceptance

Mindfulness involves being fully present in the moment and accepting your thoughts and feelings without judgment. Practicing mindfulness helps you manage stress and anxiety caused by uncertainty. Set aside time each day for mindfulness exercises, such as meditation or deep breathing. Embrace the reality of the present moment and accept that uncertainty is a natural part of life. Mindfulness enables you to respond to change with greater clarity and composure, reducing the impact of stress on your well-being.

Develop a Resilience Plan

A resilience plan outlines strategies for managing change and uncertainty. Identify potential challenges you may face and develop actionable steps to address them. Include coping strategies, support resources, and contingency plans. For example, if you're navigating a major life transition, such as a move to a new city, your resilience plan might include creating a budget, exploring local resources, and establishing new social connections. Having a resilience plan in place provides a sense of preparedness and helps you navigate uncertainties with confidence.

Embrace a Growth Mindset

A growth mindset involves viewing challenges as opportunities for learning and development. Embrace the belief that you can grow and adapt through effort and perseverance. When faced with uncertainty, focus on the potential for personal and professional growth. For example, if you encounter unexpected obstacles in your career, view them as chances to develop new skills, gain valuable experience, and build resilience. A growth mindset empowers you to approach change with optimism and adaptability.

Build a Support Network

Surrounding yourself with supportive individuals can make navigating change and uncertainty easier. Seek out friends, family members, mentors, and colleagues who offer encouragement and guidance. Share your experiences and seek advice when needed. Having a strong support network provides emotional reassurance and practical assistance during uncertain times. Engage in open communication and foster relationships that contribute positively to your well-being and adaptability.

Practice Self-Care and Stress Management

Self-care and stress management are crucial for maintaining well-being during periods of change. Prioritize activities that promote relaxation and mental health, such as exercise, hobbies, and healthy eating. Incorporate stress management techniques, such as journaling, yoga, or spending time in nature. Taking care of your physical and emotional health enhances your ability to cope with uncertainty and adapt to change with greater ease.

Stories of Women Who Have Thrived in Uncertain Times

OPRAH WINFREY: FROM Adversity to Empowerment

Oprah Winfrey's journey is a powerful example of thriving amid uncertainty. Raised in poverty and facing numerous personal challenges, Oprah transformed her life through resilience and adaptability. She embraced her experiences and used them as a platform to build a successful career in media and philanthropy. Oprah's ability to navigate uncertainty and leverage her experiences for growth exemplifies the power of embracing change and pursuing one's passions despite adversity.

J.K. Rowling: Overcoming Rejection and Failure

J.K. Rowling's story is another inspiring example of thriving despite uncertainty. Before achieving global success with the Harry Potter series, Rowling faced numerous rejections from publishers and struggled with financial difficulties. She persevered through these challenges, believing in her creative vision and continuing to write despite setbacks. Rowling's resilience and commitment to her craft ultimately led to extraordinary success, as well as a profound impact on literature and popular culture.

Malala Yousafzai: Advocating for Education in the Face of Danger

Malala Yousafzai's courage and determination in the face of danger highlight the power of embracing uncertainty for a greater cause. After surviving an attack by the Taliban, Malala continued to advocate for girls' education and women's rights, despite the risks. Her unwavering commitment to her mission and her resilience in the face of adversity have made her a global symbol of courage and advocacy. Malala's story illustrates how embracing uncertainty and pursuing a meaningful purpose can lead to significant positive change.

Sara Blakely: Turning Failure into Success

Sara Blakely, the founder of Spanx, is a testament to thriving in uncertain times through resilience and innovation. Blakely faced numerous rejections and financial challenges while developing her business. Despite these obstacles, she remained focused on her vision and persisted in refining her product and strategy. Her ability to embrace uncertainty and adapt her approach ultimately led to the creation of a highly successful company and a lasting impact on the fashion industry.

Michelle Obama: Navigating Public Life and Personal Growth

Michelle Obama's journey from First Lady to a prominent public figure demonstrates the power of embracing change and uncertainty. During her time in the White House, she navigated complex social issues and public scrutiny while remaining true to her values and goals. Michelle's ability to adapt to her evolving role and use her platform for advocacy exemplifies the strength of embracing uncertainty and leveraging it for personal and societal growth.

Actionable Tips for Embracing Change and Uncertainty

CREATE AN ADAPTABILITY Strategy

Develop an adaptability plan that outlines strategies for handling change and uncertainty. Include techniques for managing stress, setting realistic goals, and leveraging support resources. Regularly review and update your plan to reflect your evolving needs and experiences. An adaptability plan provides a structured approach to navigating uncertainty and ensures you are prepared to face challenges with confidence.

Engage in Continuous Learning

Embrace a mindset of continuous learning to stay adaptable in the face of change. Seek out opportunities for professional and personal development, such as workshops, courses, or reading. Expanding your knowledge and skills enhances your ability to respond to new challenges and adapt to changing circumstances. Continuous learning fosters resilience by keeping you informed and adaptable in a dynamic world.

Practice Positive Visualization

Positive visualization involves imagining yourself successfully navigating change and uncertainty. Spend time visualizing positive outcomes and the steps required to achieve them. This practice helps build confidence and reduces anxiety associated with uncertainty. By envisioning success and preparing mentally for challenges, you enhance your ability to embrace change with optimism and resilience.

Maintain a Flexible Routine

Establish a flexible routine that accommodates change and uncertainty while providing structure and stability. Create a daily or weekly schedule that allows for adjustments and incorporates time for self-care, goal-setting, and relaxation. A flexible routine helps you manage uncertainty by providing a sense of organization and control while allowing for adaptability.

Embracing change and uncertainty is essential for personal growth and resilience. By cultivating flexibility, focusing on controllable factors, and practicing mindfulness, you can adapt to life's unpredictability with greater ease. Building a support network and developing a resilience plan further enhance your ability to navigate challenges effectively. The inspiring stories of women who have thrived amid uncertainty serve as powerful examples of resilience and empowerment. Incorporate actionable tips such as creating an adaptability plan, engaging in continuous learning, and practicing positive visualization to build your capacity for embracing change. With these strategies in place, you can transform uncertainty into an opportunity for growth and achievement, navigating life's challenges with confidence and resilience.

CHAPTER SIX

Harnessing the Power of Generosity

Generosity and altruism are often viewed as virtues that benefit others, but they also play a critical role in enhancing personal resilience and strength. The act of giving not only enriches the lives of those you help but can also provide profound benefits to your own well-being. In this chapter, we will explore the role of altruism in personal resilience and discuss how helping others can bolster your own strength. By integrating these principles into your life, you can harness the transformative power of generosity to build a more resilient and fulfilling existence.

The Role of Altruism in Personal Resilience

Fostering a Sense of Purpose

Altruism provides a sense of purpose that is essential for personal resilience. When you engage in acts of kindness and support others, you contribute to something greater than yourself. This sense of purpose can enhance your motivation and help you navigate challenges with greater strength. For example, volunteering for a cause you are passionate about can provide a sense of fulfillment and direction, even during difficult times. Concentrating on your impact shifts your focus from your struggles to your positive impact on the world.

Building Emotional Resilience

Helping others can build emotional resilience by providing a counterbalance to personal stress and adversity. Acts of altruism can evoke positive emotions, such as happiness, satisfaction, and gratitude, which counteract negative feelings associated with stress. Research has shown that engaging in acts of kindness can lead to increased levels of happiness and reduced feelings of anxiety and depression. By fostering positive emotional experiences through altruism, you build resilience and enhance your ability to cope with life's challenges.

Strengthening Social Connections

Generosity strengthens social connections, which are crucial for resilience. Building and maintaining supportive relationships can provide a network of emotional and practical support during challenging times. When you help others, you create bonds of trust and reciprocity that enrich your social network. For instance, participating in community service or supporting friends and family in times of need fosters strong, supportive relationships that can be invaluable during your own moments of adversity.

Boosting Self-esteem and Confidence

Altruism can enhance self-esteem and confidence by reinforcing your sense of self-worth and competence. When you help others, you recognize your own capabilities and contributions, which can boost your self-image. For example, mentoring someone or sharing your expertise can affirm your skills and knowledge, leading to increased confidence. By valuing and acknowledging your ability to make a positive impact, you build a stronger sense of self and resilience.

Creating a Positive Feedback Loop

The act of giving creates a positive feedback loop that reinforces resilience. When you experience the benefits of helping others, such as improved mood and increased social support, you are more likely to continue engaging in altruistic behaviors. This cycle of giving and receiving fosters a sense of fulfillment and motivation, which contributes to your overall resilience. By creating a positive feedback loop, you enhance your capacity to navigate challenges and maintain a resilient mindset.

How Helping Others Can Bolster Your Own Strength

ENGAGE IN VOLUNTEER Work

Volunteer work is a powerful way to harness the benefits of generosity. Choose a cause that resonates with you and commit to regular volunteering. Whether it's helping at a local food bank, participating in environmental conservation efforts, or supporting a community organization, volunteering provides opportunities to make a meaningful impact and build resilience. The experience of contributing to a cause greater than yourself can provide a sense of purpose and fulfillment, enhancing your overall strength.

Practice Random Acts of Kindness

Incorporating random acts of kindness into your daily routine can bolster your own strength and well-being. Small gestures, such as offering a compliment, helping a neighbor, or donating to a charity, can have a significant impact on both the recipient and yourself. Random acts of kindness promote positive emotions, strengthen social connections, and reinforce your sense of self-worth. By making kindness a regular part of your life, you cultivate a resilient and positive mindset.

Offer Emotional Support to Others

Providing emotional support to friends, family, or colleagues can strengthen your own resilience. Actively listen, offer encouragement, and be present for those in need. By being a source of support for others, you reinforce your own capacity for empathy and compassion. This reciprocal relationship enhances your emotional resilience and provides a network of support that you can rely on during your own times of need.

Mentor or teach others.

Sharing your knowledge and experience through mentoring or teaching can enhance your own resilience and self-esteem. By guiding others and offering valuable insights, you reaffirm your own expertise and contributions. Mentoring can also provide a sense of purpose and fulfillment as you witness the growth and success of those you support. Mentoring or teaching fosters a sense of achievement and strengthens your resilience through positive impact.

Create a Generosity Ritual

Establish a ritual of generosity that aligns with your values and interests. This could involve setting aside time each week for acts of kindness, making regular donations to causes you care about, or organizing community events. By incorporating generosity into your routine, you create a consistent practice that reinforces your commitment to helping others and enhances your own resilience. A generosity ritual provides structure and purpose, contributing to a more resilient and fulfilling life.

Cultivate a Mindset of Abundance

Adopting a mindset of abundance rather than scarcity can enhance your capacity for generosity and resilience. Have faith that there is enough for everyone and that your actions can help others and yourself. Focusing on the abundance of opportunities and resources changes your perspective from limitation to possibility. This mindset encourages you to give freely and fosters resilience by promoting a positive and optimistic outlook.

Actionable Tips for Harnessing the Power of Generosity

IDENTIFY YOUR PASSIONS and Interests

To make your acts of generosity more impactful, identify causes and activities that align with your passions and interests. Consider what matters most to you and find ways to help. Focusing on your passions boosts generosity, fulfillment, and effectiveness.

Set Clear Goals for Giving

Establish clear goals for your acts of generosity, such as volunteering a certain number of hours each month, making regular donations, or supporting specific initiatives. Setting goals provides structure and motivation, ensuring that your generosity has a tangible and meaningful impact.

Track and Reflect on your Contributions

Keep track of your acts of generosity and reflect on their impact on both others and yourself. Regularly evaluate how your contributions are making a difference and influencing your own well-being. Reflecting on your experiences reinforces the positive effects of generosity and motivates you to continue.

Share Your Generosity Journey

Share your experiences and insights about generosity with others. By sharing your acts of kindness and the benefits you have experienced, you inspire and encourage others to embrace generosity in their own lives. Sharing your journey fosters a sense of community and reinforces the collective impact of altruism.

Being generous improves your life and those you help. Altruism fosters a sense of purpose, builds emotional resilience, strengthens social connections, enhances self-esteem, and creates a positive feedback loop that reinforces resilience. By engaging in volunteer work, practicing random acts of kindness, offering emotional support and mentoring, and creating a generosity ritual, you can bolster your own strength and well-being. Adopting a mindset of abundance further enhances your capacity for generosity and resilience. By integrating these practices into your life, you can harness the transformative power of generosity to build a more resilient and fulfilling existence, both for yourself and for those you support.

CHAPTER SEVEN

Rebounding from setbacks

Failure and adversity are inevitable parts of life, but how we respond to these challenges can define our path forward. Rebounding from failure implies using it as an opportunity to grow and change. This chapter explores actionable steps to recover and grow from failure and adversity, as well as inspirational stories of individuals who have overcome significant challenges. By integrating these strategies into your life, you can turn setbacks into stepping stones and emerge stronger and more resilient.

Steps for Recovering and Growing from Failure and Adversity

Acknowledge and Accept the Reality of Failure

The first step in rebounding from setbacks is to acknowledge and accept the reality of failure. Avoiding or denying the situation only prolongs the pain and inhibits growth. Accepting failure involves recognizing it as a natural and inevitable part of the journey toward success. Face the situation head-on; you lay the groundwork for recovery and can begin to address the underlying issues. For example, if you experience a business failure, acknowledge the loss and assess what went wrong without dwelling on self-blame.

Reflect and Learn from the Experience

Reflection is crucial for turning setbacks into learning opportunities. Take time to analyze the failure and identify the lessons it offers. Ask yourself questions like, What could I have done differently? What strengths and weaknesses did this experience reveal? Reflection helps you gain insights into your actions and decisions, enabling you to make informed changes for the future. For instance, if you faced a career setback, reflect on the skills and strategies that need improvement and apply these lessons to future endeavors.

Develop a Resilience Plan

A resilience plan outlines strategies for navigating and overcoming setbacks. Include specific actions to address the current challenge and prevent similar issues in the future. Your plan should encompass short-term recovery steps and long-term strategies for growth. For example, if you're recovering from a financial setback, your resilience plan might include creating a budget, seeking financial advice, and setting up an emergency fund. Having a clear plan provides direction and confidence as you work through adversity.

Set Realistic Goals and Take Incremental Steps

After acknowledging and reflecting on your setback, set realistic goals for recovery and growth. Break these goals into manageable, incremental steps to avoid feeling overwhelmed. Focus on achieving small milestones that build momentum and gradually lead to larger objectives. For example, if you're rebuilding after a failed project, start by setting goals for immediate improvements, such as revising your approach or seeking feedback. Incremental progress fosters a sense of accomplishment and propels you forward.

Seek Support and Guidance

Rebounding from setbacks often requires support and guidance from others. Reach out to mentors, friends, or colleagues who can offer advice, encouragement, and practical assistance. Surround yourself with individuals who believe in your potential and can provide constructive feedback. For example, if you're recovering from a personal setback, consider seeking support from a therapist or counselor who can help you navigate your emotions and develop coping strategies.

Maintain a Positive Mindset and Practice Self-Compassion

A positive mindset is essential for overcoming adversity and fostering resilience. Practice self-compassion by treating yourself with kindness and understanding during difficult times. Avoid harsh self-criticism and focus on maintaining a hopeful outlook. Embrace affirmations and positive self-talk to reinforce your belief in your ability to recover and succeed. For example, if you experience a setback, remind yourself of your strengths and past achievements, and affirm your commitment to growth and improvement.

Embrace Adaptability and Flexibility

Setbacks often require a shift in perspective and approach. Embrace adaptability and flexibility as you navigate through challenges. Be open to changing your plans, exploring new strategies, and adjusting your goals as needed. Adaptability allows you to respond effectively to unexpected changes and find alternative paths to success. For instance, if your initial business idea fails, be willing to pivot and explore different markets or approaches to achieve your goals.

Celebrate Progress and Achievements

Recognizing and celebrating progress is crucial for maintaining motivation and resilience. Acknowledge your achievements, no matter how small, and reward yourself for your efforts. Celebrating progress reinforces a positive mindset and provides encouragement to continue moving forward. For example, if you've made strides in overcoming a setback, take time to celebrate your accomplishments, whether through a personal reward or by sharing your success with others.

Inspirational Stories of Overcoming Significant Challenges

J.K. ROWLING: FROM Rejection to Literary Success

J.K. Rowling's journey from struggling single mother to bestselling author is a testament to resilience and perseverance. Before the success of the Harry Potter series, Rowling faced numerous rejections from publishers and battled financial hardship. Despite these setbacks, she continued to write and believe in her story. Rowling's unwavering determination and commitment to her craft eventually led to the publication of the Harry Potter books, which became a global phenomenon. Her story illustrates the power of resilience and the importance of persevering through adversity.

Oprah Winfrey: Rising Above Early Adversity

Oprah Winfrey's rise from poverty and personal trauma to becoming a media mogul and philanthropist is an inspiring example of overcoming significant challenges. Oprah faced a difficult childhood marked by abuse and financial struggles. Despite these obstacles, she pursued her passion for media and used her experiences to connect with and inspire others. Oprah's journey exemplifies the power of resilience, self-belief, and the ability to transform adversity into opportunities for growth and success.

Stephen King: Overcoming Rejection and Failure

Stephen King's path to literary success was paved with numerous rejections and setbacks. His first novel, *Carrie*, was rejected multiple times before it was eventually published. King faced financial difficulties and self-doubt during this period, but he persisted in his writing career. His perseverance paid off, leading to a prolific and successful writing career. King's story highlights the importance of resilience, determination, and the willingness to continue pursuing one's goals despite setbacks.

Malala Yousafzai: Advocating for Education despite Danger

Malala Yousafzai's courageous advocacy for girls' education in the face of extreme danger is a powerful example of resilience and bravery. After surviving an attack by the Taliban for her activism, Malala continued to speak out for education and women's rights. Her unwavering commitment to her cause, despite the threats to her life, led to global recognition and the Nobel Peace Prize. Malala's story underscores the strength of resilience and the impact of using personal adversity to drive positive change.

Nelson Mandela: From Imprisonment to Leadership

Nelson Mandela's journey from political imprisonment to becoming South Africa's first black president is a remarkable story of overcoming adversity and leading with resilience. Mandela spent 27 years in prison for his anti-apartheid activism, enduring harsh conditions and personal hardship. Upon his release, he worked tirelessly to dismantle apartheid and promote reconciliation. Mandela's resilience, leadership, and commitment to justice transformed a nation and inspired the world, demonstrating the power of perseverance and vision in overcoming significant challenges.

Actionable Tips for Rebounding from Setbacks

CREATE A RECOVERY JOURNAL

Maintain a recovery journal to document your experiences, reflections, and progress. Use the journal to track your goals, setbacks, and the steps you are taking to overcome challenges. Regularly review your entries to gain insights, celebrate achievements, and adjust your strategies as needed. A recovery journal provides a structured way to process your experiences and stay focused on your path forward.

Develop a Support Network

Build a network of supportive individuals who can provide encouragement, advice, and practical assistance during difficult times. Seek out mentors, friends, and peers who can offer valuable perspectives and help you navigate setbacks. Actively engage with your support network and reciprocate by offering support to others in need.

Set up regular check-ins

Schedule regular check-ins with yourself to assess your progress and adjust your strategies as needed. Set aside time each week or month to review your goals, reflect on your achievements, and identify any new challenges. Regular check-ins help you stay accountable, make necessary adjustments, and maintain focus on your recovery and growth.

Seek Professional Help if Needed

If you find it challenging to navigate setbacks on your own, consider seeking professional help. Therapists, coaches, or counselors can provide valuable support and guidance in processing your experiences and developing effective strategies for recovery. Professional assistance can offer new insights and tools for managing adversity and building resilience.

Rebounding from setbacks is an essential skill for personal growth and resilience. By acknowledging and accepting failure, reflecting on your experiences, developing a resilience plan, and seeking support, you can turn challenges into opportunities for growth. Inspirational stories of individuals who have overcome significant adversity illustrate the power of resilience and determination. Integrating actionable tips such as creating a recovery journal, building a support network, and seeking professional help can further enhance your ability to rebound from setbacks. Embrace the journey of overcoming adversity as a pathway to personal transformation and strength, and let your experiences guide you toward a more resilient and fulfilling future.

CHAPTER EIGHT

Living your Truth

In a world often marked by external pressures and societal expectations, living authentically can be both liberating and challenging. Authenticity involves aligning your actions and decisions with your core values and beliefs, allowing you to live a life that is true to who you are. This chapter delves into the importance of authenticity, explores how to live in alignment with your values, and offers practical exercises to help you identify and uphold your core beliefs. By embracing your true self, you can cultivate a more meaningful and fulfilling life.

The Importance of Authenticity

Fostering Genuine Connections

Authenticity fosters genuine connections with others. Living your true self attracts those who value and respect you. Genuine relationships are built on trust, honesty, and mutual respect, all of which stem from living authentically. For instance, when you express your true thoughts and feelings, you create an environment where others feel comfortable doing the same, leading to deeper and more meaningful connections.

Enhancing Personal Fulfillment

Living authentically leads to greater personal fulfillment. When your actions align with your values, you experience a sense of harmony and satisfaction that comes from being true to yourself. This alignment allows you to pursue goals and passions that resonate with your inner self, leading to a more fulfilling and purposeful life. For example, if you value creativity, engaging in creative pursuits will bring a sense of joy and accomplishment that aligns with your core beliefs.

Building Resilience and Confidence

Authenticity builds resilience and confidence by reinforcing your sense of self-worth and identity. When you stay true to your values, you develop a strong foundation that supports you through challenges and adversity. This inner strength fosters confidence and self-assurance, allowing you to navigate life's ups and downs with greater ease. For instance, when you make decisions that reflect your authentic self, you build confidence in your ability to stay true to your beliefs and navigate obstacles with integrity.

Promoting Personal Growth

Living authentically promotes personal growth by encouraging self-reflection and self-awareness. Being in touch with your core values makes you more likely to pursue growth-promoting activities. Authenticity requires introspection and a willingness to explore your true self, leading to continuous personal evolution and a deeper understanding of who you are. For example, embracing your true interests and passions can lead to new opportunities for learning and growth.

Exercises to Identify and Uphold Your Core Beliefs

VALUES DISCOVERY EXERCISE

Begin by identifying your core values, which are the fundamental beliefs that guide your actions and decisions. Start by listing values that resonate with you, such as honesty, compassion, or creativity. Reflect on past experiences and consider which values were most important to you during those times. To further clarify your values, ask yourself questions like: What principles guide my decisions? What qualities do I admire in others? Use this exercise to create a list of your top five core values that reflect your true self.

Values Alignment Check

Once you've identified your core values, assess how well your current actions and decisions align with them. Review various aspects of your life, such as your career, relationships, and personal goals. For each area, ask yourself: Are my actions consistent with my core values? If not, what changes can I make to align more closely with my beliefs? This alignment check helps you identify areas where you may be deviating from your values and provides a roadmap for making the necessary adjustments.

Authenticity Journaling

Engage in authentic journaling to explore and express your true self. Set aside time each day to write about your thoughts, feelings, and experiences related to living authentically. Use prompts like, What does living authentically mean to me? When have I felt most true to myself? What challenges have I faced in staying authentic? Journaling allows you to gain insight into your values and experiences, helping you stay connected to your true self and identify areas for growth.

Vision Board Creation

Create a vision board that reflects your core values and aspirations. Gather images, quotes, and symbols that represent your values and desired future. Arrange them on a board or digital platform to create a visual representation of your authentic self. Use your vision board as a daily reminder of your values and goals, and refer to it when making decisions or setting new objectives. A vision board helps you maintain focus on what truly matters to you and reinforces your commitment to living authentically.

Authenticity Assessment

Conduct a self-assessment to evaluate how well you are living in alignment with your values. Create a list of key areas in your life, such as career, relationships, and personal interests. For each area, rate your level of alignment with your core values on a scale of 1 to 10. Identify areas where you are doing well and areas where improvements are needed. Use this assessment to set specific goals and action steps for increasing alignment with your values.

Accountability Partner

Partner with someone who shares similar values and goals to support each other in living authentically. Share your core values and aspirations with your accountability partner, and establish regular check-ins to discuss your progress and challenges. Provide mutual encouragement and constructive feedback to help each other stay true to your values. An accountability partner can offer valuable support and motivation, making it easier to maintain authenticity in your daily life.

Practice Mindfulness and Self-Reflection

Incorporate mindfulness and self-reflection practices into your routine to stay connected to your authentic self. Engage in activities such as meditation, deep breathing, or mindful journaling to cultivate self-awareness and clarity. Mindfulness helps you tune into your inner thoughts and feelings, making it easier to identify and uphold your core values. Use these practices to regularly check in with yourself and ensure that your actions are aligned with your beliefs.

Set Authentic Goals

Set goals that reflect your core values and aspirations. Ensure that your goals are meaningful and aligned with what matters most to you. For example, if creativity is a core value, set goals related to pursuing artistic projects or exploring new creative outlets. By setting authentic goals, you create a clear path for living in alignment with your values and achieving personal fulfillment.

Inspirational Stories of Living Authentically

ELEANOR ROOSEVELT: Champion of Human Rights

Eleanor Roosevelt's life is a testament to living authentically in alignment with her values. As a First Lady, she used her platform to advocate for human rights, social justice, and gender equality. Roosevelt's commitment to her core values led her to champion causes such as the Universal Declaration of Human Rights and women's rights. Her unwavering dedication to her principles, despite facing opposition and criticism, exemplifies the power of living authentically and making a meaningful impact on the world.

Steve Jobs: Pursuing Passion and Innovation

Steve Jobs' journey as a visionary entrepreneur highlights the importance of authenticity and following one's passions. Jobs was known for his relentless pursuit of innovation and his commitment to creating products that aligned with his vision of excellence. Despite facing setbacks and challenges, he remained true to his core values of creativity and quality, leading to the creation of groundbreaking products such as the iPhone and Macintosh. Jobs' story illustrates the impact of living authentically and pursuing one's passions with unwavering dedication.

Malala Yousafzai: Advocating for Education

Malala Yousafzai's advocacy for girls' education in the face of extreme adversity exemplifies living authentically and courageously. After surviving an attack by the Taliban for her activism, Malala continued to speak out for education and women's rights with unwavering determination. Her commitment to her core values of education and equality, despite facing significant danger, led to global recognition and the Nobel Peace Prize. Malala's story demonstrates the power of staying true to one's beliefs and making a difference in the world.

Brené Brown: Embracing Vulnerability and Courage

Brené Brown's work as a researcher and author focuses on the importance of authenticity, vulnerability, and courage. Brown's research on topics such as shame and vulnerability has empowered individuals to embrace their true selves and live authentically. Her own journey of sharing personal stories and insights in her books and TED Talks reflects her commitment to living in alignment with her values. Brown's story highlights the impact of embracing vulnerability and authenticity in personal and professional life.

Living your truth involves embracing authenticity and aligning your actions with your core values. By recognizing the importance of authenticity, engaging in exercises to identify and uphold your core beliefs, and drawing inspiration from those who have lived authentically, you can cultivate a more meaningful and fulfilling life. Practical steps such as value discovery, authenticity journaling, and creating a vision board provide actionable ways to stay true to yourself and make decisions that reflect your true self. Embrace the journey of living authentically, and let your values guide you toward a life of purpose and fulfillment.

CHAPTER NINE

Cultivating a Growth Mindset

Agrowth mindset is a powerful tool for fostering resilience and achieving personal and professional success. This concept, popularized by psychologist Carol Dweck, emphasizes the belief that abilities and intelligence can be developed through dedication and hard work. Embracing a growth mindset can transform how you approach challenges, setbacks, and opportunities for improvement. This chapter explores the essence of a growth mindset, its impact on resilience, and practical strategies to cultivate a mindset geared toward continuous improvement.

Understanding the Growth Mindset and Its Impact on Resilience

Defining a Growth Mindset

A growth mindset is characterized by the belief that your abilities are not fixed traits but can be developed through effort, learning, and perseverance. Individuals with a growth mindset view challenges as opportunities to grow, believe that their skills can improve over time, and are more likely to embrace feedback and learn from failures. This contrasts with a fixed mindset, where individuals believe their abilities are static and unchangeable. Understanding this distinction is crucial for leveraging the growth mindset to enhance resilience and personal development.

Impact on Resilience

Resilience is the ability to bounce back from adversity and maintain a positive attitude in the face of challenges. A growth mindset significantly impacts resilience by fostering a proactive approach to overcoming obstacles. When you view setbacks as temporary and surmountable rather than as reflections of your limitations, you are more likely to persevere and adapt. For instance, if you encounter a setback in your career, a growth mindset encourages you to view it as a learning opportunity and seek ways to improve, rather than seeing it as a sign of failure.

Developing Problem-solving Skills

Individuals with a growth mindset are more inclined to engage in problem-solving and creative thinking. They approach challenges with curiosity and a willingness to explore different solutions. This proactive approach enhances their ability to tackle problems effectively and find innovative solutions. For example, when faced with a complex project, a person with a growth mindset will experiment with various strategies and seek feedback to refine their approach, ultimately leading to better outcomes and increased resilience.

Fostering a Passion for Learning

A growth mindset nurtures a love for learning and self-improvement. Individuals with this mindset are motivated by the process of learning itself rather than solely focusing on outcomes. They are more likely to pursue new skills, seek knowledge, and embrace lifelong learning. This enthusiasm for learning contributes to personal growth and adaptability, which are essential components of resilience. For instance, if you are passionate about acquiring new skills, you are more likely to stay engaged and motivated, even when faced with challenges.

Practical Ways to Foster a Growth Mindset

EMBRACE CHALLENGES

Actively seek out and embrace challenges as opportunities for growth. Instead of avoiding difficult tasks, approach them with a mindset of curiosity and determination. Embracing challenges allows you to stretch your abilities and develop new skills. For example, if you are given a challenging project at work, view it as a chance to learn and grow rather than as an obstacle. This shift in perspective can increase your confidence and resilience when tackling complex tasks.

Cultivate a Love for Learning

Engage in activities that stimulate intellectual curiosity and personal development to foster a love of learning. Pursue hobbies, take courses, and explore new areas of interest. By consistently seeking opportunities for learning, you reinforce the belief that growth and improvement are ongoing processes. For instance, if you have an interest in a new field, enroll in a class or attend workshops to deepen your knowledge and skills.

Set Process-Oriented Goals

Focus on setting process-oriented goals rather than outcome-based ones. Process-oriented goals emphasize the steps and strategies you will take to achieve success, rather than solely focusing on the end result. This approach encourages continuous improvement and reinforces the idea that progress is made through effort and persistence. For example, if your goal is to improve your public speaking skills, set specific objectives such as practicing regularly, seeking feedback, and refining your techniques.

Emphasize Effort and Persistence

Shift your focus from innate talent to the importance of effort and persistence. Celebrate the hard work and dedication that contribute to success, rather than attributing achievements solely to natural ability. Acknowledge and reward yourself for the effort you put into overcoming challenges and achieving goals. For instance, if you work diligently to improve your skills in a particular area, recognize and appreciate your efforts as a key factor in your progress.

Seek Feedback and Learn From Criticism

Embrace feedback and view criticism as an opportunity for growth. Instead of taking feedback personally, approach it with an open mind and a willingness to learn. Constructive criticism provides valuable insights into areas for improvement and helps you refine your skills. For example, if you receive feedback on a project, analyze the suggestions provided and use them to make improvements. This approach fosters a growth mindset by demonstrating that feedback is a tool for development rather than a judgment of your abilities.

Practice Self-Compassion

Cultivate self-compassion by treating yourself with kindness and understanding when facing setbacks or failures. Avoid harsh self-criticism and instead focus on constructive self-talk. Recognise that making mistakes is a natural part of the learning process, and that self-compassion promotes resilience and growth. If you fail, remember that it's a learning experience, and that your mistakes don't define you.

Celebrate Small Wins

Acknowledge and celebrate small victories and milestones along the way. Recognizing and appreciating incremental progress reinforces the idea that growth is a continuous journey. Celebrating small wins boosts motivation and confidence, encouraging you to keep pushing forward. For instance, if you achieve a minor goal in a larger project, take time to celebrate your accomplishment and reflect on the progress you've made.

Surround Yourself with a Growth-Oriented Community

Build a supportive network of individuals who share a growth mindset. Engage with people who encourage and inspire you to pursue your goals and embrace challenges. Surrounding yourself with a growth-minded community provides motivation, support, and accountability. For example, join groups or communities related to your interests and goals, where you can connect with like-minded individuals who value continuous improvement and learning.

Reflect on your Growth Journey

Regularly reflect on your personal growth journey and the progress you have made. Take time to review your achievements, challenges, and lessons learned. Reflecting on your experiences helps reinforce a growth mindset by highlighting your development and the impact of your efforts. For instance, keep a growth journal where you document your experiences, insights, and progress toward your goals. Use this journal to track your evolution and celebrate your successes.

Inspirational Stories of Embracing a Growth Mindset

THOMAS EDISON: INNOVATOR and Inventor

Thomas Edison's journey as an inventor exemplifies the power of a growth mindset. Edison faced numerous failures and setbacks during his pursuit of creating the light bulb. Despite repeated experiments that did not succeed, he viewed each failure as a learning opportunity and persisted in his efforts. Edison's resilience and dedication eventually led to the successful invention of the light bulb, demonstrating the impact of a growth mindset on achieving groundbreaking innovations.

J.K. Rowling: Overcoming Rejection

J.K. Rowling's path to success with the Harry Potter series is a testament to his growth mindset. Before achieving literary fame, Rowling faced multiple rejections from publishers and struggled with personal challenges. She continued to revise and submit her manuscript, driven by her belief in the value of her work. Rowling's persistence and dedication ultimately led to the publication of the Harry Potter books, illustrating how a growth mindset can overcome obstacles and lead to extraordinary achievements.

Michael Jordan: The Pursuit of Excellence

Michael Jordan's career in basketball highlights the importance of a growth mindset in achieving excellence. Despite being cut from his high school basketball team, Jordan used the setback as motivation to improve his skills. His relentless work ethic, commitment to practice, and belief in his ability to grow led to an illustrious career and numerous accolades. Jordan's story underscores the significance of persistence, effort, and a growth mindset in reaching the pinnacle of success.

Oprah Winfrey: Overcoming Adversity

Oprah Winfrey's rise from a challenging childhood to becoming a media mogul exemplifies the power of a growth mindset. Despite facing significant adversity and personal struggles, Winfrey embraced opportunities for growth and learning. Her resilience, dedication, and belief in her ability to overcome challenges contributed to her success as a television host, entrepreneur, and philanthropist. Winfrey's journey illustrates how a growth mindset can transform adversity into opportunities for personal and professional growth.

Cultivating a growth mindset is a transformative approach to enhancing resilience and achieving continuous improvement. Understanding the principles of a growth mindset, embracing challenges, focusing on effort and persistence, and seeking feedback can help you cultivate a mindset that supports personal growth and success. Inspirational stories of individuals who have embraced a growth mindset demonstrate the profound impact of this mindset on overcoming obstacles and achieving greatness. Implementing practical strategies such as setting process-oriented goals, practicing self-compassion, and surrounding yourself with a supportive community will help you develop a growth mindset and unlock your full potential. Embrace the journey of growth and improvement, and let a growth mindset guide you toward a more resilient and fulfilling life.

CHAPTER TEN

Thriving Amid Chaos

In an ever-changing world marked by uncertainty and unpredictability, the ability to thrive amid chaos is a crucial skill. Chaos, whether in the form of personal crises, professional upheavals, or global events, can challenge our sense of stability and well-being. However, by mastering techniques for maintaining calm and clarity and applying resilience skills in everyday life, you can not only navigate chaos effectively but also emerge stronger and more adaptable. This chapter delves into practical strategies for thriving in tumultuous situations and explores how to apply resilience skills in real-life scenarios.

Techniques for Maintaining Calm and Clarity in Chaotic Situations

PRACTICE MINDFUL BREATHING

Mindful breathing is a powerful technique for regaining composure and clarity in chaotic situations. Focusing on your breath can help you calm your nervous system and center your thoughts. To practice mindful breathing, find a quiet space and take slow, deep breaths in through your nose, allowing your abdomen to expand. Exhale slowly through your mouth. As you breathe, focus solely on the sensation of your breath entering and leaving your body. This simple practice helps reduce stress and anxiety, allowing you to approach chaotic situations with a clearer mind.

Adopt a Grounding Technique

Grounding techniques help anchor you to the present moment, which can be especially useful during times of chaos. One effective method is the 5-4-3-2-1 technique, where you identify:

✓ **5 things you can see:** Look around and identify five objects in your environment.

✓ **You can touch four things:** You can feel the texture of the objects.

✓ **You can hear three things:** Pay attention to the sounds around you.

✓ **2 things you can smell:** Identify scents, if any.

✓ **1 thing you can taste:** Focus on a taste or simply the sensation in your mouth. This exercise helps shift your focus from overwhelming emotions to tangible, immediate experiences, providing a sense of calm and control.

Maintain a Positive Inner Dialogue

Your internal dialogue plays a significant role in how you manage chaos. Cultivate a positive and supportive inner voice by challenging negative thoughts and reframing them constructively. For instance, if you're facing a work crisis, instead of thinking, "I can't handle this," reframe it as, "This is challenging, but I have the skills to navigate it." Positive self-talk boosts your resilience and reinforces your ability to handle chaotic situations with confidence.

Establish a Routine

During chaotic times, maintaining a sense of normalcy through routine can provide stability and predictability. Establish a daily routine that includes regular activities such as exercise, meal times, and relaxation. Consistent routines help manage stress by providing structure in the midst of uncertainty, creating a sense of order. For example, even during a demanding work period, set aside time each day for a walk or meditation to maintain your well-being.

Set Priorities and Focus on What You Can Control

In chaotic situations, it's essential to identify your priorities and focus on aspects within your control. Create a list of tasks and responsibilities, and categorize them by urgency and importance. Concentrate your efforts on tasks that align with your priorities and address what you can influence. Let go of tasks or concerns beyond your control to avoid unnecessary stress. For example, if you're dealing with a sudden change in project deadlines, focus on completing high-priority tasks first and delegate or postpone less critical activities.

Utilize Visualization Techniques

Visualization techniques can help you manage chaos by mentally preparing for and navigating challenging situations. Visualize yourself successfully handling the chaos with calm and confidence. Picture yourself taking deliberate actions and making clear decisions. This mental rehearsal enhances your preparedness and reduces anxiety. For example, before a high-stakes meeting, visualize yourself speaking clearly, addressing challenges effectively, and handling any unexpected issues with poise.

Engage in Physical Activity

Physical activity is a proven stress reliever and can help maintain clarity during chaotic times. Engage in regular exercise, such as walking, jogging, or yoga, to release endorphins and reduce tension. Exercise also improves cognitive function and emotional regulation, enabling you to approach chaotic situations with a clearer perspective. For instance, incorporating a daily workout into your routine can help you stay centered and focused, even in high-pressure circumstances.

Seek Social Support

Connecting with others provides emotional support and practical assistance during chaotic times. Reach out to friends, family, or colleagues for encouragement, advice, or simply a listening ear. Social support helps alleviate stress and provides a sense of solidarity. Share your experiences and concerns with trusted individuals who can offer perspective and reassurance. For example, discussing a challenging situation with a supportive friend can provide valuable insights and alleviate feelings of isolation.

Real-Life Applications of Resilience Skills in Everyday Life

MANAGING THE WORK-LIFE Balance

Applying resilience skills to manage work-life balance involves setting boundaries and prioritizing self-care. Create a clear distinction between work and personal time, and establish boundaries to prevent work from encroaching on your personal life. Use techniques such as mindful breathing and positive self-talk to manage stress and maintain balance. For instance, if you're working long hours, schedule regular breaks and engage in activities that recharge you, such as hobbies or spending time with loved ones.

Navigating Personal Relationships

Resilience skills are valuable in navigating personal relationships, especially during conflicts or challenges. Practice active listening, empathy, and effective communication to address issues constructively. Apply techniques such as grounding and positive self-talk to manage your emotions and approach conflicts with a calm and open mindset. For example, during a disagreement with a partner, use mindful breathing to stay centered and focus on understanding their perspective rather than reacting impulsively.

Adapting to Life's Transitions

Life transitions, such as moving to a new city or changing careers, can be chaotic and stressful. Apply resilience skills by embracing a growth mindset and viewing transitions as opportunities for growth. Set realistic goals, seek support from others, and maintain a positive inner dialogue to navigate the transition effectively. For instance, if you're starting a new job, focus on building relationships, learning new skills, and staying adaptable to the changing environment.

Handling Financial Uncertainty

Financial uncertainty can create significant stress and chaos. Use resilience techniques to manage financial challenges by creating a budget, setting financial goals, and seeking advice from financial experts. Practice mindful breathing and positive self-talk to alleviate anxiety about financial concerns. For example, if you're facing financial difficulties, develop a plan to address your expenses and seek support from financial advisors or support groups to navigate the situation effectively.

Coping with Health Challenges

Health challenges, whether personal or related to loved ones, can be overwhelming. Apply your resilience skills by focusing on what you can control, seeking medical advice, and practicing self-care. Engage in physical activity, maintain a healthy diet, and use techniques such as visualization and grounding to manage stress. For instance, if you're managing a chronic health condition, work with your healthcare provider to develop a treatment plan and incorporate stress-relief practices into your daily routine.

Pursuing Personal Goals

Applying resilience skills to achieve personal goals involves setting clear objectives, overcoming obstacles, and staying motivated. Use techniques such as setting process-oriented goals, celebrating small wins, and seeking support from others to stay focused and resilient. For example, if you're working toward a fitness goal, create a plan that includes regular workouts, track your progress, and reward yourself for achieving milestones.

Managing academic or career pressures

Academic or career pressures can create chaos and stress. Apply resilience skills by organizing your tasks, setting priorities, and seeking support from mentors or peers. Practice techniques such as mindful breathing and positive self-talk to manage stress and maintain focus. For instance, if you're facing a challenging academic deadline, break the task into manageable steps, stay organized, and use stress-relief techniques to maintain clarity and productivity.

Thriving amid chaos necessitates mastering techniques for maintaining calm and clarity, as well as applying resilience skills in everyday life. By practicing mindful breathing, adopting grounding techniques, and fostering a positive inner dialogue, you can navigate chaotic situations with composure and clarity. Real-life applications of resilience skills, such as managing work-life balance, navigating personal relationships, and coping with life transitions, demonstrate the value of these techniques in various aspects of daily life. Embrace the strategies outlined in this chapter to build your resilience and thrive in the face of uncertainty and change. By developing these skills, you can transform chaos into opportunities for growth and emerge stronger, more adaptable, and empowered.

CHAPTER ELEVEN

The Pathway to Empowerment

Empowerment is the process of gaining control over your life and making choices that align with your true self. It is a journey that transforms challenges into opportunities for growth and harnesses resilience to build a fulfilling and purposeful life. This chapter explores actionable steps to transform challenges into opportunities for growth and provides strategies to maintain and build upon the resilience you've developed. By understanding and implementing these concepts, you can pave your own pathway to empowerment and live a life characterized by strength, purpose, and continuous growth.

Steps to Transform Challenges into Opportunities for Growth

Shift your Perspective

The first step in transforming challenges into opportunities is to shift your perspective. Instead of viewing challenges as insurmountable obstacles, reframe them as opportunities for growth and learning. Adopting a positive mindset allows you to approach difficulties with curiosity and openness rather than fear and resistance. For example, if you encounter a setback in your career, view it as a chance to acquire new skills or reevaluate your goals rather than as a personal failure. This shift in perspective empowers you to tackle challenges with a proactive and optimistic attitude.

Set Clear Goals and Action Plans

Once you've redefined your challenges as opportunities, establish clear goals and action plans to address them. Break down your challenges into manageable steps and set specific, measurable, achievable, relevant, and time-bound (SMART) goals. Create an action plan that outlines the steps you need to take to achieve these goals. For instance, if you're facing a financial challenge, set a goal to create a budget, reduce expenses, and explore additional income sources. An actionable plan provides direction and motivates you to take consistent steps toward overcoming your challenges.

Develop Problem-solving Skills

Enhancing your problem-solving skills is crucial for transforming challenges into opportunities. Cultivate a systematic approach to problem-solving by identifying the root cause of the issue, brainstorming potential solutions, evaluating the pros and cons of each solution, and selecting the best course of action. Practice critical thinking and creativity to generate innovative solutions. For example, if you're dealing with a project that's falling behind schedule, analyze the underlying issues, explore ways to streamline processes, and implement strategies to get back on track. Effective problem-solving empowers you to overcome obstacles and achieve your goals.

Embrace failure as a learning opportunity

Failure is an inevitable part of growth and transformation. Instead of fearing failure, embrace it as a valuable learning opportunity. Analyze what went wrong, extract lessons from the experience, and use that knowledge to improve and adapt. For example, if a business venture doesn't succeed, assess the factors that contributed to the failure and apply the insights to future endeavors. Embracing failure with a growth mindset enables you to learn from mistakes, build resilience, and approach future challenges with greater confidence and insight.

Seek Support and Collaboration

Don't hesitate to seek support and collaborate with others when facing challenges. Surround yourself with a network of mentors, peers, and allies who can offer guidance, feedback, and encouragement. Collaboration fosters diverse perspectives and solutions, enhancing your ability to navigate challenges effectively. For instance, if you're working on a complex project, seek input from colleagues or industry experts to gain valuable insights and support. Building a supportive network empowers you to leverage collective knowledge and resources to overcome obstacles and achieve your goals.

Cultivate Emotional Intelligence

Emotional intelligence (EQ) is the ability to understand and manage your own emotions while empathizing with others. Developing EQ enhances your resilience and ability to navigate challenges with grace. Practice self-awareness by regularly reflecting on your emotions and reactions, as well as developing self-regulation strategies to manage stress and maintain composure. For example, if you experience frustration during a difficult situation, use mindfulness techniques to calm yourself and respond thoughtfully. Cultivating emotional intelligence empowers you to handle challenges with emotional resilience and empathy.

Celebrate Progress And Achievements

Acknowledge and celebrate your progress and achievements, no matter how small. Recognizing your accomplishments reinforces your sense of empowerment and motivates you to continue pursuing your goals. For instance, if you achieve a milestone in overcoming a challenge, take time to celebrate and reflect on the progress you've made. Celebrating your successes reinforces positive behaviors and provides encouragement to keep moving forward on your path to empowerment.

How to Maintain and Build upon the Resilience You've Developed

CONTINUOUSLY SET AND Pursue New Goals

Maintaining resilience involves continually setting and pursuing new goals that align with your evolving aspirations. As you achieve your goals and overcome challenges, establish new objectives that push you to grow further. Regularly setting and pursuing goals keeps you focused, motivated, and engaged in your personal and professional development. For example, after completing a major project, set new goals that challenge you to acquire additional skills or explore new opportunities. Continuous goal-setting ensures ongoing growth and strengthens your resilience.

Practice Self-care and Well-Being

Prioritize self-care and well-being to sustain your resilience over time. Engage in activities that promote physical, emotional, and mental health, such as regular exercise, healthy eating, relaxation techniques, and hobbies. Self-care practices replenish your energy, reduce stress, and enhance your overall well-being, enabling you to face challenges with renewed strength. For instance, incorporate self-care routines into your daily schedule, such as practicing mindfulness, engaging in creative activities, or spending time with loved ones. Maintaining self-care practices ensures you remain resilient and balanced in the face of ongoing challenges.

Reflect on your Journey

Regularly reflect on your journey to assess your progress, challenges, and growth. Reflecting on your experiences helps you recognize patterns, learn from past experiences, and celebrate achievements. Reflection is a tool for self-assessment and continuous improvement. For example, set aside time each month to review your goals, evaluate your progress, and identify areas for growth. Reflection provides valuable insights into your resilience and helps you adjust your strategies for continued success.

Stay Adaptable and Open to Change

Resilience is closely linked to adaptability and openness to change. Embrace change as an opportunity for growth, and remain flexible in your approach to challenges. Adaptability enables you to navigate evolving circumstances and seize new opportunities. For instance, if a project or goal requires adjustments, be willing to modify your plans and strategies to align with changing conditions. Staying adaptable ensures you remain resilient and capable of thriving in dynamic environments.

Build on your Strengths

Leverage and build upon your existing strengths to enhance your resilience. Identify your core competencies and areas of expertise, and find ways to apply them to new challenges and opportunities. Building on your strengths boosts your confidence and effectiveness in navigating obstacles. For example, if you excel at problem-solving, use this skill to tackle complex issues and seek innovative solutions. By capitalizing on your strengths, you reinforce your resilience and capability.

Seek Ongoing Learning and Development

To continue to build your resilience, commit to ongoing learning and development. Pursue opportunities for professional and personal growth, such as training programs, workshops, and educational resources. Lifelong learning enhances your skills, knowledge, and adaptability, contributing to your overall resilience. For instance, enroll in courses related to your field or explore new areas of interest to expand your expertise. Ongoing learning ensures you stay current and capable of handling new challenges effectively.

Foster Positive Relationships

Nurture and maintain positive relationships with supportive individuals who contribute to your resilience. Surround yourself with people who encourage your growth, provide constructive feedback, and offer emotional support. Positive relationships enhance your sense of belonging and provide valuable resources for navigating challenges. For example, engage in regular interactions with mentors, friends, and colleagues who uplift and inspire you. Cultivating positive relationships reinforces your resilience and fosters a supportive network.

Embrace a Growth Mindset

Continue to cultivate a growth mindset by embracing challenges, learning from failures, and pursuing continuous improvement. A growth mindset reinforces your belief in your ability to develop and adapt, enhancing your resilience. For instance, when faced with a new challenge, approach it with curiosity and a willingness to learn rather than fear of failure. Embracing a growth mindset ensures that you remain resilient and empowered in the face of evolving circumstances.

The path to empowerment entails transforming challenges into opportunities for growth, as well as maintaining and building upon the resilience you've developed. By shifting your perspective, setting clear goals, developing problem-solving skills, and embracing failure as a learning opportunity, you can effectively navigate challenges and unlock your potential. Maintaining resilience requires continuous goal-setting, self-care, reflection, adaptability, and leveraging your strengths. By implementing these strategies, you empower yourself to thrive amid adversity and create a life marked by strength, purpose, and ongoing growth. Embrace the journey of empowerment, and let each challenge be a stepping stone on your path to a fulfilling and empowered life.

IN SUMMARY

The Next Steps in your Journey

Now that your journey of discovery and personal growth is over, reflect on what you've learned and look ahead. There is no endpoint to the road to empowerment and resilience; rather, it is a continuous journey replete with chances to grow and prosper. This conclusion includes inspiring and motivating thoughts, a review of the key lessons addressed throughout the book, and words of encouragement for what's to come. Strength, resilience, and fulfillment will be yours to keep expanding as you apply these lessons to your everyday life.

Important Points Review

Awakening to One's True Potential

Understanding oneself is the cornerstone of personal progress. Through approaches such as self-reflection and discovering your inner qualities, you've learned how to unearth your own potential. Embrace the activities that lead you to a better understanding of your fundamental principles and areas of interest. This self-knowledge can help you live your true self.

Nurturing Self-Love

Self-love is vital for establishing resilience and having a positive mindset. By practicing self-compassion and positive self-talk, you've learned how to treat yourself with care and respect. Remember to prioritize self-care and reinforce your values periodically. Cultivating self-love increases your emotional base, helping you to confront obstacles with confidence and grace.

Building Your Inner Fortress

Developing mental and emotional fortitude is vital for managing life's obstacles. By applying tactics to build your resilience and developing a solid support structure, you've prepared yourself to manage stress and setbacks successfully. Maintain and reinforce your inner fortress by continuing to improve your problem-solving abilities, seeking help, and practicing self-care.

Embracing Change and Uncertainty

Life is unpredictable, and accepting change is vital to personal progress. Techniques such as focused breathing, flexibility, and recognizing obstacles as opportunities have enabled you to confront uncertainty with a resilient attitude. Apply these tactics to stay adaptable and open to new experiences, converting chaos into avenues for development.

Harnessing the Power of Generosity

Altruism not only helps others but also bolsters your own resilience. By participating in acts of kindness and generosity, you've learned how to boost your well-being and establish important relationships. Continue to be generous in your daily life and recognize its impact on your strength and the community.

Rebounding from Setbacks

Overcoming failure and hardship is a vital element of progress. You've learned strategies to recover from setbacks, including assessing shortcomings, learning from them, and moving on with fresh drive. Embrace failures as chances for learning and progress, and utilize them as stepping stones toward bigger successes.

Living your Truth

Authenticity and harmony with your values are important to having a meaningful life. By discovering and keeping your essential values, you've learned how to live in conformity with your genuine self. Continue to focus on your principles and ensure that your behaviors and choices correspond with your real selves.

Cultivating a Growth Mindset

A growth mindset helps you perceive problems as opportunities for constant progress. You've examined practical approaches to cultivating this mentality, including accepting learning and being adaptive. Apply these ideas to continually pursue personal and professional progress, and embrace each problem with curiosity and resilience.

Thriving Amid Chaos

Maintaining calm and clarity in chaotic conditions is crucial for successful problem-solving. Techniques such as focused breathing, defining priorities, and seeking social support have allowed you to manage turbulence with serenity. Utilize these tactics to remain grounded and focused, even in the face of overwhelming situations.

The Pathway to Empowerment

Transforming problems into opportunities for development and preserving resilience are keys to empowerment. By defining clear objectives, developing problem-solving skills, and building upon your talents, you've learned how to harness your potential and create a satisfying existence. Embrace these ideas as you continue to pursue your goals and manage your path with empowerment and confidence.

Encouragement for the Ongoing Journey

As you go ahead on your path, remember that development and empowerment are constant processes. Life will provide new problems and opportunities, and your capacity to adapt and prosper will rely on the resilience and insights you've learned. Embrace each event as an opportunity to better enhance your talents and capabilities.

Stay devoted to your self-discovery and personal improvement. Regularly review the routines and approaches that have resonated with you throughout this book. Whether it's participating in self-reflection, practicing self-love, or fostering a development mindset, these tools will serve as useful resources on your road to empowerment.

Surround yourself with a friendly group that supports your progress and celebrates your triumphs. Seek mentors, allies, and friends who share your beliefs and objectives. Their encouragement and input will help you remain motivated and aligned with your objectives.

Be patient with yourself, and remember that progress is a journey, not a destination. Celebrate your achievements, no matter how gradual, and use setbacks as a chance to grow and improve. Your resilience and strength will continue to increase as you negotiate the twists and turns of life with bravery and drive.

Inspirational Final Thoughts

Your path ahead is a monument to your strength, resilience, and dedication to personal progress. As you embrace empowerment, realize you can design your future. The obstacles you confront are opportunities in disguise, and your capacity to convert adversity into progress is a measure of your inner strength.

Believe in your power to accomplish greatness and have a positive effect on the world around you. Your path is unique, and every step advances you. Trust in your ability, remain loyal to your principles, and continue to follow your interests with unshakable persistence.

In the face of uncertainty, let your resilience be your guiding light. Embrace change with confidence, use the power of giving, and remain consistent in your quest for authenticity and progress. Your path is a continual experience, loaded with possibilities to flourish, inspire, and empower yourself and others.

As you walk ahead into the future, bring with you the information and insights you've learned. Your route to empowerment is lighted by your commitment to progress, your fortitude to tackle obstacles, and your desire to live a life of purpose and satisfaction. Embrace the path ahead with optimism and confidence, knowing that you have the power and resilience to conquer any barrier and realize your ambitions. Your path ahead is a tribute to your immense potential and the endless opportunities that await you.

WORKBOOK

Harnessing Resilience in Turbulent Times

Introduction

Welcome to the companion workbook for "Empowered Through Chaos: Harnessing Resilience in Turbulent Times." This workbook is designed to help you apply the principles and strategies discussed in the book to your own life. Each chapter contains exercises, reflections, and actionable steps to guide you on your journey to resilience and empowerment.

Chapter 1: The Power of Self-Discovery

Exercise 1: Self-Reflection Journal

Take 10–15 minutes each day to write about your thoughts and feelings. Focus on moments that made you feel strong, proud, or fulfilled. Reflect on what these moments reveal about your core strengths and values.

Exercise 2: Identifying Strengths

List five strengths you believe you possess. Ask close friends or family members to share what they believe are your strengths. Compare these lists and reflect on any commonalities or surprises.

Chapter 2: Nurturing Self-Love

Exercise 1: Daily Affirmations

Write down three positive affirmations about yourself. Repeat these affirmations each morning to start your day with a positive mindset.

Exercise 2: Self-Care Checklist

Create a checklist of self-care activities that nurture your mind, body, and spirit. Aim to incorporate at least one activity from each category into your weekly routine.

Chapter 3: Building Your Inner Fortress

Exercise 1: Support System Map

Draw a map of your support system, including friends, family, mentors, and other key figures. Identify any gaps and think about ways to strengthen these connections.

Exercise 2: Resilience Planning

Develop a personal resilience plan. Identify potential stressors and outline strategies to manage them, including relaxation techniques, problem-solving approaches, and who you can turn to for support.

Chapter 4: Embracing Change and Uncertainty

Exercise 1: Change Acceptance Journal

Write about a recent change in your life. Consider how to turn your initial reaction into a learning opportunity. What did you learn from this experience?

Exercise 2: Adaptability practice

Identify a small, manageable change you can make in your daily routine. Practice adapting to this change and reflecting on the experience at the end of the week.

Chapter 5: Harnessing the Power of Generosity

Exercise 1: Acts of Kindness Log

Commit to performing at least one act of kindness each day. Keep a log of these acts, and reflect on how they make you feel and how they impact others.

Exercise 2: Volunteer Planning

Research local volunteer opportunities that resonate with your values. Choose one to participate in, and reflect on how helping others strengthens your own resilience.

Chapter 6: Rebounding from Setbacks

Exercise 1: Failure Analysis

Think of a recent setback or failure. Write a detailed analysis of what happened, what you learned, and how you can apply these lessons moving forward.

2: Resilience Story

Write about a time when you overcame a significant challenge. Highlight the strategies you used and the strengths you discovered in the process.

Chapter 7: Living Your Truth

Exercise 1: Core Values Assessment

Identify your top five core values. Assess your lifestyle against these values and consider how you can live more authentically.

Exercise 2: Authenticity Challenge

Choose one area of your life where you feel you are not fully authentic. Take steps to align your actions with your true self and reflect on the outcomes.

8: Cultivating a Growth Mindset

Exercise 1: Growth mindset reflection

Think about a recent challenge or mistake. Reflect on how you can view it as an opportunity for growth, and what steps you can take to improve.

Exercise 2: Learning Goals

Set three learning goals for yourself. Outline a plan to achieve these goals, including the resources you need and milestones to track your progress.

Chapter 9: Thriving Amid Chaos

Exercise 1: Stress Management Techniques

Practice mindfulness techniques such as deep breathing, meditation, or progressive muscle relaxation. Reflect on how these practices help you maintain calm in chaotic situations.

2: Daily Gratitude

Write down three things you are grateful for each day. Reflect on how focusing on gratitude helps you maintain a positive perspective, even in challenging times.

Chapter 10: The Pathway to Empowerment

Exercise 1: Goal Setting

Identify a major goal you want to achieve. Break it down into smaller, actionable steps, and set a timeline for completing each step.

....

Exercise 2: Reflective Practice

Regularly reflect on your progress towards your goals. Adjust your strategies as needed and celebrate your achievements, no matter how small.

....

Conclusion: Your Journey Forward

Exercise 1: Personal Manifesto

Write a personal manifesto that encapsulates your values, goals, and commitment to resilience. Refer to this document regularly to stay motivated and focused on your journey.

....

Exercise 2: Future Vision

Imagine your life five years from now. Write a detailed description of your desired outcome, accomplishments, and resilience journey.

....

Final Thoughts:

Remember, this workbook is a companion on your journey to resilience and empowerment. Use it as a tool to guide your growth, reflect on your experiences, and celebrate your progress. Your journey forward is a testament to your strength and potential. Embrace it with confidence and courage.